What do you think?

A collection of poems by Catherine Balavage

For Luke. All of your dreams can come true.

Forward by Margaret Graham.

I've long thought Catherine Balavage is an extraordinarily accomplished young women: author, writer, editor and actor, mother, wife, and she can add **poet** to that roll of honour.

In *What do you think?* a collection of her poems written throughout her still young life, she connects with the vast majority of the human race, as she writes of the struggle to achieve a sense of who a person is, the efforts to release oneself from early angst and stand tall; finally achieving confidence potential and contentment. In her introduction Catherine says that *As an artist it sometimes feels like you are born without skin, yet spend your life rolling around on razor blades.* Well, quite.

In What do you think? Catherine has written poems that could be songs - I could hear music. She has written poems beating time with the rhythm in her head, poems hauled up from experience, observation and unflinching, sensitive thought.

A triumph.

Introduction.

So here it is. A book of my poetry. A part of me thought I was mad putting a book of my poetry together. Maybe no one would be interested, or think it was lame. But I did not get where I am in life by worrying about what other people think about me. My writing career started precociously. I wasn't even a teenager when I first started sending my work to editors. At first it was all rejection letters, but then something happened: someone said yes. I have always felt that is the essence of life; lots of work and rejection, finally followed by success and happiness. Nothing comes easily. Some days, not even the words do. But when I was a teenager I was as prolific as I was relentless. I always loved reading but I was less sure of my writing. I knew I loved it and that was what I wanted to do with my life. Writing was like breathing, *but was it good.*

The truth is, not all of these poems will be good. Many of them left me unsure whether or not to put them in. I made sure there are no bad ones, but others I left solely because I liked the message, or I thought it was interesting to see how my writing evolved. How my voice changed as I got better and I practiced more, gaining confidence.

Confidence first came when an English teacher loved my poem, Tigress, Tigress, so much that he not only made me stand up and read it out loud for all of the class, but also said I should get it published. I was very ill when I was at school. Glandular fever was followed by a post-viral thing. I won't bore you with stories of ill health, but the teacher told me to come to school more. He got upset because he said I could be a good writer. He said I had *potential*. In truth, it is all any child needs to hear. I have never stopped writing since. I don't think any teenager is particularly articulate and I was no exception. I found it hard to tell people how I was feeling, so I would write a poem and then show them instead.

I haven't edited many of these poems, and many of them were written when I was a teenager. In fact, I was in a band when I was younger and many of them started off as songs. I remember one music executive saying that they 'reminded him of Paul McCartney'. That helped spur me on too. I stopped writing poetry for many years after being told by unsupportive people that it was 'uncool' and 'boring'. Stupid them, silly me. I would never let anyone stop me doing anything now, but that is the wisdom that comes with age. You cannot be a writer without putting yourself out there and being vulnerable. To be a writer, a good writer, you have to give yourself, your experience, thoughts and emotions into your words. That is not to say they are all autobiographical, but they are products of their environment. I have had a few people make the mistake of thinking that something I had written was true, or a part of me. Sometimes with bad consequences. This makes putting yourself out there harder. It is always hard being criticised. As an artist it sometimes feels like you are born without skin, yet spend your life rolling around on razor blades. But bravery is important and putting your work into the world to be criticised is brave. Which brings us to this book. I hope you like the poems, but if you don't, I tried.

The idea of publishing a book of my poetry percolated for a while, but it was my mother who nudged me on. So here it is. The beginnings of my writing career. I hope you like this book. Enjoy the poems and please let me know via Twitter @Balavage *what you think*.

Thieves.
When women are mean girls
Motherhood.
Hell to this war.
One mistake is all it takes.
Loved person.
It is just life.
Sweet little princess.
Hear lies.
Night.
No way out.
Why?
Got to be true.
The Untold Truth.
Breaking.
Do not need your words.
After years love.
Some people call it love.
The way it has got to be.
Love in four lines.
Living, surviving and dying happily.
Colour of love.
Do I live?
Scared.
They.
The wonders in my head.
If.
An impromptu celebration poem.
Indirectly.
The cost of your soul
One kind.
Boy blue.
Light.
Harder.
Emotions.
I have a need.
In my life.
Not able.
I remember my wedding day.
Rules.
Trying hard.
In this world.
My loveless world.
Loves young dream.
Exhaustion.
Between me and the ghosts in my heart.
The dead and the living.
Unknown facts of life.

Love.
What I ain't.
Alright.
And I want.
Kids.
Say goodbye.
See you cry.
Do you know? Do you care?
I do not, I do.
I try.
I want you.
Do not want to be good.
My rat.
A to Z.
A human puppet.
This is the meaning of life.
New feelings.
Gods children.
Times.
I could.
Jim Daley.
Not Today
Moving
On the dark side.
Party.
Bad love.
The not knowing.
Make way.
Self destruction.
The problem with humans.
The silencer.
Along the way.
Courage.
Trauma conditioning.
I did not give birth to her so she could die like this.
Memoirs of a Fake Women
Tigress, Tigress.
Self involved people.
When you lose a loved one.
Don't Cry Child.
Poetry.
What I want in my life.
You only notice when things are wrong.

Thieves

Littered broken hearts
One million men
Tearing me apart
Vestiges of
What I used to be
Leaving behind
All different parts of me
Traces
Chunks
Bits
Intellectual property
All stolen from me
And I will never be complete again
And the waiter came around with decapitated roses

When women are mean girls

Another barb
To bring a smile to your face
You think it wounds
Not quite
But I will confess it grates
How a woman can act like a mean girl
Time and time again
Her insecurity and bitterness
Coming out in bitchy comments

I guess I should feel sorry for you
That your life has led you to this
Vile and wrapped up in your own bitterness
But woman like you give women a bad name
Lashing out, attacking, trying to cause pain

I know you just don't like my happiness
That it causes you pain
That your jealousy is like your other face
Sneering, ugly and plain

I take it as a compliment
That you can't just keep quiet
That you cannot become the adult you are
That you have to let your hate perspire

I move on, of course
And I smile as I do
Because although you bore me and disappoint me
I am happy, because I am nothing like you

(This was written in 2016. I wish it wasn't as relevant as it is. I do have to point out that men can be bitchy too, but sometimes it just hurts more when it comes from another woman).

Motherhood

They say that after this I will be a woman
But I feel I already earned that long ago
Long before the waves and the pain
My dues long paid up
Unlike those other dues
This one will be worth it

They say this will change me.
And it irks me that they are not wrong
One bouncing baby
To change the melody of the song

Half a stone of giggles and crying
To bring a joy
That could bring back the dying

Hell to this war

I am still living in this great hell
Falling asleep to police car sirens
Crying as time comes to a standstill
Ringing inside me, warning bells

I am living inside this great war
With my cold heart at the other side of my locked door
Crying as the dead cat calls
Telling me it is now or not at all
For I am at war with this great hell

One mistake is all it takes

The grey shirt on my back says 'County Jail'
I was young in the mind
And I bought a one-way ticket to hell
Now there is no way
I will ever get out of here

I think of my mother, my father, my son
All of the people I have let down
Because of all my wrongs
But I must do my penance now
Before I can make everything right
Before I can see the respect return in their eyes

I am just a number now
A statistic in a book
With a debt to pay to society
Days that will become years
Years into decades
Decades that I will miss
As my son grows up without me
Becomes an adult
An adult, I pray, who won't be like me

The grey shirt on my back says 'County Jail'
I was young in the mind
And I bought a one-way ticket to hell
Now there is no way
I will ever get out of here

Loved person

Broken promises I knew you could not keep
You only ever tried to love me and in gratitude I lay at your feet
Because I was in love too, but my love was different

My love was the notion of life, a good one
All I wanted from ear to ear; a smile from my own mouth
It did not work
You loved me so selflessly I could not leave
Although I know now it was only through your love for me that I loved you
You lost your own identity
You chose mine but I wanted mine to keep

Still. Here I am
This time only crying at your ever loving feet
I owe you too much to leave
So for the rest of my life. If I never find the courage
I will be the living, loved dead
Even though I see
Your love in an otherwise cruel world binds me
Forgive me. I doubt for all that I was ever worthy

It is just life

How many times do I have to cry before you put your arms around me?
Too many hearts I have had to break
Till you finally said you're glad you found me
Did you mean it?
I am so tired of being human. Tired of breaking down

There is so much pain inside me now
I wonder if I will ever turn around
I will never be able to do it on my own
It is taking so much of my strength
Trying to find a home just to love in

Sweet little princess

Sweet little princess who loved playing with her dolls
Got caught in the cross fire of it all
Now sweet little princess is away
No longer able to play
And when the sweet little princess got to heaven she asked God, "Why did
you let man invent that weapon?"

Out playing one day
Children only ever want to play
Full life ahead. Not now, no longer
Sweet little princess is dead
And there she once lay in a hospital bed
Tears from her mother's eyes
Making the blanket wet

Hear lies

Stone cold broken heart
I knew it was never a good idea to love you but we could never be apart

I could pick myself up again
Give as well as take
But I just don't have another heart left for you to break

The night I saw grow
We could never be something else
Instead we hated and turned in on ourselves
Pain was all we ever had

Night

This night forever has a new meaning
Right now I am not sure if this is the future I am seeing

Well, this night love has a new meaning
This is not happiness I am feeling
From this night on love has a new meaning
From this night on my heart is always going to be screaming

All through breaking the silence of this cold, cold night
This night you have no idea how bad I am feeling

No way out

No way out
And I turn and take a step
But you push me further back
I land hard breaking into pieces
And I say, "Child, dear child why do you cry?"
She turned around and said, "My spirit has died
I have hit teens, I hit twenty, I hit thirty, I hit forty, I hit fifty, I hit sixty
I hit dead
Nothing of me left
Child no more
Nothing no more
Because I didn't try
All gone
Can't carry on"

I am trapped
It is all closing in around me
The pressure is closing down on me
I need something to hang onto but nothing is there
Everything is worse for wear
All the clutter, all the mess. I am finding it hard to do my best
I need a rest but I can't. It is a waste of time
I want to know why I am always scared. Where is my security?
Why am I scared of me and what is deep within me?

Why?

What did I do wrong?
What didn't I do right?
I thought you were the love of my life
Why do you want to go?
Want to go away
When I have so much left to do and say?

Got to be true

Thinking about you lying here
I need to face the thing I most fear
Tears streaming down my face
I feel like the only person in the human race.
That has hurt so bad
I was in love
But love never lasts

I need to lift myself up
I need to look up
Life isn't that bad
I am young and free
I am on the prowl for someone better than you
I am going to be in love
Love has got to be true
True, but not with you

I thought life was a piece of cake but sadness keeps me awake
Awake from my sleep
Awake from the things I most need
Love is such a dangerous thing
Sometimes you win but mostly lose
Lose control and get the blues
Do not know what to do
Because love is your control

The Untold Truth

You know it is hard never knowing where you are
Never giving me the loving that I need
All I want is some commitment but you never say you love me
It is the untold truth that is making me hurt
The endless nights wondering where you are
The untold truth. Cutting me up
And you, never giving me love

I thought all the promises were true but I have gone out with a million other
men like you
I should have known from the start
It is the good-looking ones that break your heart

I know the smart thing to do is give up on you
Stop the tears
Forget the fears, but my heart screams out for love

It is all over now
Except the getting over you

Breaking

In brief boy you have messed me up
Messed me up bad
Because I always pictured us together forever
We did not even make it to November
Now my illusions are shattered
Nothing even matters

Do not try to suck me in with your petty little words
"Sorry" just isn't going to ease this hurt
I do not understand how it turned out so bad
Although I knew it had to end
You gave me the line about being friends

Now I am alone
Yet still feeling strong
But I knew it would not last long
The lies went on and on

Do not need your words

Did you mean every twisted word?
Was it really me you meant to hurt?
Left me in the lurch
In the dark
No hope. No light. No security.
Lost without you to help me find my way

Evil words hissing in my ear
Last thing I want to hear
Now it hurts when you are here and when you're not

Unlike you I have nothing to say
I have been like that since we went our separate ways
To be honest
I do not want you to say anything either
It will just bring back all those tears that you left me
Like a mother torn away from a sick newborn baby

If your heart was as big as your mouth
I would be having the time of my life but that is not possible
Nothing works out
Nothing capable
Like a dozen lamps but not enough money for bulbs
Got ten pence
But that is not enough

After years love

The world comes crashing down
A broken heart is found
A smile on a little girl's face
After so many years, replaced
A full stop removed, Happiness
At last shining through

The blackness of life
With a light shined on it
Desperation with a glimmer of hope
Love that will not let go
Clinging on still

A forgotten thing remembered again
What you hope
Shocks you when it finally comes through
Is it right to be this happy?
What is happening?
Could this love possibly still be you?
I never thought four
Would come out of my two and two
A light like you

Some people call it love

You made me feel like a contaminated lake you did not want to swim in
Just wash your feet with me
I will pretend not to see
Although your "love" blinds me anyway
Only my heart knows how much you hurt me
My head should know better

The way it has got to be

Some say what needs to be needs to be
No matter your insight
Life repeats bad history
Nobody seems to be looking to the future except me
I am trying and I just cannot see why some people be so blind
They just wait out time

I wait for my time. Working hard so my time comes
For in some other distant place I will get my call
Because when good comes, bad falls
I do not listen when they say "That is the way it has got to be"
Because God gave me two eyes to see

Love in four lines

I never thought, I never knew, that I would meet someone like you
Someone who would make my life complete
Make me go weak at the knees, but now forever and ever again
You will be the only man for me

Living, surviving and dying happily

I was born in a little town and died there seventy years later
I did nothing in my life but survive
And as I was old and dying
I had nobody in my life
Nobody missed me in death
Except a cat I used to feed

But I am not sad
Do not cry for me tonight
I am one of the many billions of people who quietly help the world go around
Just living out my quiet life and dying softly in my sleep
Seventy years later

Colour of love

Blue became the colour of death
Breath lost beneath the waves
Brown became a symbol of the end and black
Lowering as the two colours became one
Then the green grass grew over you
Becoming your freedom and mine
As I bring white, red and pink flowers to you every weekend
I love you my freak

Do I live?

My life could be a distant dream
I could be lazy, getting fat and busting out of my seams
But I will not and yet, I do not know how

Life cannot be "All of that" for me
And yet, I hope I am wrong

I am human in being scared
Human in my failure
But am I too human so that I am consumed by my fear?

Scared

I am not scared of life
I am just scared
Because when the darkness comes crawling
Taking everything in its path
It sends shivers up my back and I feel like I am being attacked

I put my shields up armed to disarm
But everything backfires
Then everybody, even me, backs out
The cowards

I think I know what I am scared off
I am scared of you
Because I don't know what to do to get you to stay
I am scared you will go away

I am scared. I am scared to live. I am scared to die
I am scared when the darkness comes
I want my man safe from harm in his arms
But I am scared

They

They tell me to learn but they won't teach me
They tell me they love me
Then they leave me
They want to do good until you run out of money
And no matter what they say
You know nobody love you

The wonders in my head

I worshipped your god
I was down on my knees
Did he give me something?
I just find it so impossible to see
If I had believed from the start
Do you think he would still hurt me?
If I had shown a little faith
Maybe he would have been able to love me

Is there a father above me?
I find it so impossible to see

If

If my heart burns for you does that mean it is gently on fire?
When you're gone is the flame smouldered and the black smoke that engulfs
my heart smothering it painfully?

Is that why I not only long for you obsessively when you're gone but also
when you're not as near as I want?
Maybe that is why I can never leave?
My heart reminds me you keep the fire in my flame burning
The answer is yes
Please stay
I will love you always

An impromptu celebration poem

Haters gonna hate
Bitches gonna bitch
Whiners gonna whine
I don't give a f**k, because I have wine.

(This one was not written when I was a teenager. It was written in August 2016 when I finished the first draft of this book. Surprisingly, wine was not actually involved).

Indirectly

I sit in my room with my broken heart
Unable to let my happiness re-start
One man saw me. Another man told
Then in their hearts. My love would not unfold
So they stood up and took up
Went away with a bit each of my broken heart
So now how can my happiness re-start?

The cost of your soul

How much does your money cost?
Did you, like so many, gain success instead of love?
Losing your mind in a disillusioned society
The use of prozac is up higher everyday

Did your son wear trainers to your father's funeral?
Did they not tilt their hats when the limo passed the pub?
You got angry when someone cut you up at the traffic lights
Teenagers listening to techno, stoned high in someone else's car
Just how are you different from them?
Twenty silk cuts and a few whiskeys, some wine everyday
I heard a rumour there is no love in the world today
Please don't make them right
Or is it all out of your hands?

One kind

If you do not go with your kind then people treat you like dirt
You're weak and stupid if you wear a skirt
If you do not believe in God then you're nothing at all

We are all born the same way
We are all different in many ways
We are all one kind
We are all equal

If you have not got balls you're nothing at all
An attitude is lethal if you're a girl
So take it to the next level
Make sure people do not go through hell
Appearances should not be judged
You should give life all you got
We are all equal
Yes, even you

Boy blue

I am human
I make mistakes
A normal person who can break
But now I am lost
I used to think when our love was young that you were the only one but I was
wrong
You are not the one

Looking into the future I feel so blue
Wondering what to do
How can I handle life without you
Life with someone new

Time is the only cure but right now I feel like I am going to cry forever more
Hurt and lonely I lie in bed
Because I just can't get you out of my head
I know I should call my friends but I want to be alone
I just can't face the fact you are gone

I will get over you in time but at this moment
I just can't get you out of my mind

(I did worry about how much the younger me wrote poems about men and
love. The feminist in me almost took some out, but I wrote many of them as
songs, and I see nothing wrong with wanting to find love. Even men want
that.)

Light

A forgotten thing remembered again
What you hope
Shocks you when it finally comes through
Is it right to be this happy?
What is happening?
Could this love possibly still be you
I never thought four
Would come out of my two and two
A light like you

Harder

I know you do not love me
So do not bother cuddling me
Do not ask me how I am feeling
I am feeling nothing at all
I do not know what I am doing
This is driving me up the wall
Tell me do you care at all?
These days you are getting harder to believe
I feel stupid when it is you and me
Maybe for once I will do this your way but things get worse between us
everyday

Why are you punishing me?
There is nothing I have done wrong
I think it would be better if you were gone
Are you true to me?
Some evidence is all I need to get me on my feet
Do not hurt me again. I can't hurt anymore
I don't know what is happening. It's all a blur
But I tell you in this world
I am not getting far

Emotions

Happy, happiness
Hasn't always been a friend of mine
Now I want to feel it all the time

Sad, sadness
I have forgotten what it means
I am going to erase all the sadness I have seen

Love, loving
Is something I have never felt before because the only thing a man ever
showed me was the door
But not anymore

Now I know the score
I am not going to say I will start again
The past is still there
It will not go away
So I will live with it
Be happy again

I have a need

Sometimes I feel and sometimes I am nothing
Sometimes all I need is your loving, but you will not love me
You do not even cuddle me
Can you not see I am still your little girl?
What I need is your love
If not, the worlds

In my life

In my life there is a shadow, some depth
But I have not found any reasons yet
In my life someone is watching over me, and I wish they would leave me be
In my life there ain't much and I don't know the meaning of luck
That is not a reason for giving up
Three words "Live it up."

Not able

I have not got any tears left to cry and I am too young to die
I just wish I knew
What separates someone like me from someone like you?
What has life got against me? Why can't I be free?
My body is wracking with pain. In my eyes you can see the strain
Now someone has took away the air so I can't breathe
I am lying on the floor not able to see

Say you wish me well but really you wish me hell
Well I am sick of hanging with you
Mind your own business, leave me alone
Pretend you're trying to help me but you make my suffering go on
Marvin Gaye once sang to me. His songs made me happy
Now he is gone like everything else

I remember my wedding day

The day I got married I remember it so clearly
My family in the church
Crying in their Sunday best
Full of joy
Celebrating my husband and my new beginning

It was a staged event
The beginning of an end and a false fairytale
My happiness died with my freedom
Now my marriage is dead
I can't understand why my family are not here
Mourning in their black suits
Yet celebrating the end that has caused my new beginning and new
happiness
Not the end, but the start

(This was written in 1999. Long before my own wedding in 2014).

Rules

Well do I qualify into your sick stereotype?
Where you need to be trendy or you don't fit in
Where you cannot step out of line and you just cannot win

Judge you like a jury and like a jury, they are not always right
But still they go on the first sight

Trying hard

In my life I never go up
Stays the same, drinking out the same cup
Always going down and it is showing on my face
I wish all my life would erase
But I will keep on going
Even though I don't want to
I will keep on going and I might find love
Something to dream of

I am going to find someone to be sincere to
In love with me
In love with you
One day that will be the line that I use

Life is really hard and you get more and more scars
That hurts more than anything else by far

In this world

Everybody following each other. Human guinea pigs.
Routine freaks nine to five. Never been what I am about.
Never been a backseat girl because to be heard you need to shout.
In this world everybody is different but everyone is the same.
In this world there is over 8 billion brains.
But for what we do with them we do not even need them.
Waste of intelligence.

In this world pollution. In this world revolution.
This world was once a green place. Now it is just a grey face.
Building homes over woods when there are empty homes down the road.
All the scams. Never told what we want to be told.
Being rejected because we are too young or old.
In this world so much wrong.
In this world not, going to last long.

My loveless world

Even though you said we are through I want to go back for one last look.
At how it used to be. You and me.

Without you I am so lonely
Cannot explain how I feel
Cannot believe this is real

I cry because you broke my heart
Why is it just my little world that has stopped?
I cry because you are not here
It hurts worse when you are near

The world is not going to stop but without you
I am lost
The sun will still shine but it will be dark in my life
Until you're mine

Loves young dream

I feel your touch inside me
I feel your passion
I can tell your love for me is everlasting
Now up is the only way for our love
Now I have to give loneliness up

So look deep into my eyes anytime a doubt should arise
Now I know love is above all else
We are loves young dream

Exhaustion

You call me up five times a day
I just don't understand how anyone can have so much to say
Especially when you're self-absorbed and it's all about you you you
I used to laugh at all your unfunny jokes
But now I know you were fake before you even spoke
I used to think you were so intelligent
You were just sprouting words from all those books you read
But reading and doing are two different things
And I won't let your agenda against me win

Between me and the ghosts in my heart

I never meant to love him
Have his message on my phone
I never meant to fall
I wanted to be left alone
I'm scared for my ambitions though they will never be gone
But I never meant to love him
I was happy being alone

The dead and the living

There are those who die and those who live
The pain and anguish and leaving behind are all that is in-between
We think we deserve what we want in life, but we no more deserve the things
we want in life
Than we do a swim in a shark-infested pool
But life always gets the better of us
It takes our dreams and crushes them
Our loved ones and lets them die

We go on and persevere in some way
Becoming who we are more and more as what we once loved us lets us go
Sometimes it was a false misconception you never wanted anyway
So you have your career and your house and yourself and your family and
your pets
You have everything that goes with living and not much of anything else.
And then you wonder where it went
Become
Ancestors looming, as a new generation makes its way in the world

Unknown facts of life

I feel like throwing myself against the wall
Living on the edge I am not afraid to fall
Because I have already been through it all

Love

Too many things were happening
I just did not see
I did not believe in love
So I did not realise what you meant to me

What I ain't

Indestructible is what I am not
When illness comes
I feel the pain
Knocks me for six
Makes me sick

Sometimes the emotional is harder than the physical
You feel like you always fall
You need someone there when you call
You want a life. That's all

Alright

It is near the end
I am happy again
I have been through a lot of emotional and physical hurt
But now I am going to give all that up
Nobody else is going to treat me like dirt

And I want

I do not want children on the street
Nowhere to eat and sleep
I want children hanging with their mates
Making something of themselves before it is too late

I want everything to be alright
I want everyone to see the light
Bring out the person within
I promise you
Work hard, Then you'll win

(I almost didn't put this one in. It is not a brilliant poem, but I liked the message and I was only twelve when I wrote it. I have always been socially conscious and aware that confidence and opportunity are what the young need to make something of their life, no matter their social class).

Kids

I am not like the other kids
All the other kids do is play
I am not like all the other kid.
I have something to say
I am not like all the other kids
I do everything my way

Say goodbye

I know you're going to say goodbye and I know why

You called me at 1am saying you would be late again
I just don't know what to do
That women can't keep her hands off you
Then you say you're going out with the boys
You're treating me like some old toy

I know you're going to leave me soon
I am not sure what to do
But I will not get on my knees and beg you to stay
Because that is not my way

At one point you were all I had to live for but not anymore
Now there are a million other reasons to live for
I will find them, as I head out the door
Say goodbye

See you cry

I never saw a tear in your eye until that day
Never thought I would need to take your tear away

I walked away did not turn around
I never thought silence was so loud
Never meant to hurt you, sorry anyway
I did not mean to hurt you even though I walked away
I hope one day you can forgive me

Do you know? Do you care?

Do you know how it feels to starve to death?
For no one to care?
To never have a rest

Do you know what it is like to never have anything?
To never have a life
And wake up in pain in the middle of the night.
Do you know how it hurts?
When someone rubs your face in the dirt
Do you really care?
When there are wars breaking out everywhere?

I do not, I do.

I don't want to live
I don't want to die
I don't want to run away because
I don't want to say goodbye
I know I will find something in my life

I do want family
I do want friends
I do want to stay and live my life until the end
I know my hurt will mend
Life is so confusing

I do
I do not
I am confused
I did
I didn't
What is the use?
Do this
Did not do that
This is a pain
That is good
That is bad
When will it end?

I try

Feeling kinda lonely walking down the street
Try to keep my head up but I end up staring at my feet
I try to do some good
Try to do my best
But how can I get results
If there isn't a test

I want you

I am in love with you
I do not know what to do
To make you love me too
You're in love with her. I am in love with you
I wish you would say you loved me too
It's hard watching you kiss her
I wish it was me
Watching you cuddle her
I have to flee
Crying myself to sleep at night
The only thing that keeps me alive
Is the thought of you and me

Love is such a dangerous thing
From the heart it comes from within
In love it is hard to win
Because love is not always equal from both people
Jealousy can cause the end
Now my heart cannot mend
I will pull through in the end
One day I hope it will be you and me
That one day I will be happy

Do not want to be good

I want respect
I want dignity
I want a life beyond this rat race
I want to change the way you think
I am never going to change
I do not want to be a good girl because good girls die young
I want to have a lot of fun

My rat

I put my trust in your hands
I gave you my heart with mine
I let you make the decisions in my life
You gave me a promise

I never let you down
I let you go on all those holidays
I promised you I loved you
And you lied to me

You asked for my forgiveness
You begged for me again
You told me you could not live without me
I said goodbye and never hurt again

A to Z

How much it hurt
It was my heart I was giving up
It was you who was tossing it around
Now it is in the lost and never again found

Right through A to Z
I know everything you've done off the top of my head
Always being cruel
My heart drowned in the love pool because of you

I was down everyday. You always had to have your way
Forgot my birthday every year
Good times? I never had them
I had a date with the television or my tears

Right through A to Z you were pulling my leg
Breaking my heart
Tossing it around

A human puppet

So you say it is today
Your sanity has returned
You love me more than ever
Only by now. You would think I would have learned
And it happens again
I am a human puppet on your string
One day I will find the strength but I never seem to want to win

Little tides hit us
Swimming in your lake
I will not let go of my life jacket
I know you would let me drown and I am sick of getting wet
I am not the kind of girl that is just okay with the concept of drowning in your
pool
Even puppets can break free from strings
Lets not ever start that process again

This is the meaning of life

We are not making it. Just being oh so faking it
To kill. Not to kill
Was not me I was not there
I did. Did not ruin everything
Was not me. It was you

Struggling everyone in the world to get by
Wars about religion but all worshipping the same guy
Sexist this whole world and let's not even mention love
Hypocritical. Something happens in the ghettos
Some official says something must be done
Then he goes home where he get everything he wants
Unfair this world to a T. Everybody looking but they can't see

Do not judge until you hear the full story because in this world you have to
search for the glory
So quick to judge. Not so quick to show love
You got it all but you're all messed up
All the same but you're not listening. Ignore me again

I could give you a word of advice but you're too wrapped up in your own life
Not realising I am not being personal
Not realising I am just trying to get through to you
Well everyone else and I are sick of making do
This is the end. Happiness is through
All like a language with no words. Dying to be heard
The devil rejected our soul because we feel too young or old
Breaking relationships of a hundred years
Crying all these tears. Oh all the fears

New feelings

What is going on in my mind?
What are these things in my head I am trying to hide?
Not wanting to show
These things I do not want to know

I thought I just liked you
I ignored all the feelings
I was so blind. Loving you without seeing

Always were friends now when I look at you
There is something there that I never thought could be
Since I love you and you tell me you love me. You be Romeo. I will be Juliet
We will rewrite Shakespeare's book and give it a happy ending

(I find this poem of teenage love quite sweet. Alas, there was no boy it was
written for. I was quite the ugly duckling when I was at school).

God's children

People say things that really hurt but I don't think we should be any different
just because we wear a skirt
Or our skin is black, white or both
You have no reason for hurting our feelings
I am no different

I thought we were all God's children so tell me if you can
What makes a women? What makes a man?
If we are black, white or both. Our race should not be a joke

Time and time again we get put down by people
I hope they change
We can stand on our own but we still need to feel loved and adored
We need more
We are human beings like you. We need love too

Times

Sometimes I get the blues
I do not know what to do,
But only when I am not with you
Sometimes I feel alone
Not having any strength to carry on
But that is only when you are gone

I could

I don't know if I want you back
One day I turned around and you were gone
I found it hard to carry on. Now you want me back
I don't know if I can take the chance of getting hurt again
I tell you I am sick of men

I could get back with you
But are you true?
It could never last
Just like in the past
I could end up getting hurt due to you treating me like dirt
But could is a big word
And so is love

And what do you do when you have got no one to love?
No one to be sincere to. No one to hug
No one in your life because life isn't full of love
Love is understated
I have no control of my heart when it falls in love

I will not look back because that is behind me
I wish everyone would leave me be
To the best of my ability
Some people stretch me too far
Too far then I scar
The scar of love fades in time
Love ain't true. Not this time

What?

What did I do wrong?
What didn't I do right?
I thought you were the love of my life
Why do you want to go?
Want to go away
When I have so much left to do and say?

Jim Daley

I walked into the hospital room
There is old Jim Daley sleeping in the bed again
He hasn't got anywhere else to go
He can't handle life
He is dying
but dying slow

There he goes
Security carrying old Jim Daley out the door
Even if he had a home
He wouldn't know where to go
Old Jim Daley can't get in no door

He can't handle life
And life never knew what to do with him
Structure and rules
Only overwhelmed him

He will be there every day
Even months from now
Like a moth to a flame.
Old Jim Daley finding peace in that hospital bed

Not Today

I get a feeling I should sleep my life away
I just cannot fight today
I go back and forward and all the rest
I feel real down
Find solace in bed
Anything other than that is a mystery

Moving

Twenty-five to three in the morning
I just can't get to sleep
My head is spinning. No one else is awake
I close my eyes again, but this feeling I can't break

It is because I am going away, but hopefully I will see you some other day
I am moving, but I do not want to go
Want to stay here, because this feels like home

I have been with you guys so many years and I know when I go I will not be
able to hold back the tears
That in will creep all the fears

I am moving to a new place. New directions I will have to face
Gone is the past
But then, I never thought it would last
Yes it's cause, it's because I am going away
But do not worry, I will come back some day

On the dark side

You cannot live inside the dream. She died
As if I did not already know that already
It was written in fate
Etched in life. And confirmed in death
Then say thank you
And now forever goodnight
Bye

The pain used to bear down on me
Visions of what I used to be
Now I sit and watch TV
Life isn't what it used to be
But still I get up
Sometimes I just get up to get knocked down
My life, life going
Around and around
Maybe now happy to be
Sad and happy life is to be

Party

It might be my party but I feel like I am dying
It really is crowded but I am on my own
I might be the reason this party is happening but none of them are here for me
I am alone at my party
Not even I know me

Bad love

Was I so mad to think my dreams might come true?
Was I restored with faith only for it to be snatched away?
Stand up to be shot down
It is against the law to be happy in your town

Even now I think it's a dream and then I feel like crying
For a second
I reach out and grab you
Until I see that hate in your eyes that I have never seen before
I wrote this just so you know that I'll never understand

The not knowing

I got two pounds in my pocket and millions of ambition
I got a life and an inability to live it
I'm looking for a leader
Just so I can climb
Don't want to be stuck in a hole forever
I know there is more to life

Make way

Make way for sorrow
Right now I'm living for tomorrow
Or maybe even the next day
Because my heart is screaming mayday
Please take away my pain
And kiss me gently
Says the sub conscious to the conscious

I can't cry
Even though in my heart
My world dies

Self-destruction

Smoke yourself into a shallow grave
Where you can still breathe and live there captivated
Not able to be sure on your feet. And then you leave me
Grey.
You called me on Friday to apologise
After a week of me crying myself to sleep
Once again you worm your way in
And I start the whole hurting process all over again
The worst of opposite

The problem with humans

People say the war in Kosovo is over
I doubt it very much
Religion religion and more religion.
They say we're all worshipping the man up above
We say, "why God?" and ask him out loud for help
But why should he come down from heaven to hell
When we brought it all on ourselves

The silencer

You're not here to kill me
You are here to murder every word I said
You can't comprehend me so will shoot me down
What you don't believe
Can't believe
But do fear
Your silencer on your gun is not that
My words are already in the air

Along the way

All the old clichés are still there
Night turns into day
Everything is the same as it was
With little changes along the way

The world just keeps on spinning
As though it could not care less
The humming birds keep singing
The young fly out the nest

Still I know you will be there for me
Just like some people call the ocean the sea

I am wearing white
It is my wedding day
My mother is weeping; my father proud, gives me away
We will be happy
Waking up to the same face everyday
With life's little changes and some babies along the way

This poem was written on 25.04.2000.

Courage

I travelled when I was too scared to leave the front door
When I was uncomfortable I said more
When the insecurity was killing me I pretended I was everything I ever wanted to be
I did everything
Everything, but be little timid, shy, introverted me

Trauma conditioning

I'm scared
Everything is messed up in my head
I remember nothing at all
Except that everything that ever was killing me was fake
It was all
Trauma conditioning and poor judgement

I did not give birth to her so she could die like this.

I did not give birth to her for her to be found dead in some dirty flat in
Bothwell
I did not love her so drugs could pump into her body, killing her in her
sixteenth year
I did not work my fingers to the bone so she could die confused, scared and
alone
I did not give birth to her so she could just die like that

Memoirs of a Fake Women

I left your ordinary life
Cut our band
A freeing knife
I broke your heart
To get on with my life

I never loved you
You gave me your heart
I kept mine with bars around it
I never lied to you
It was always going to be this way
There is nothing. Of the women you love here
Don't assume that I care
She never existed anyway

Tigress, Tigress

She lies on the ground
Silent as night
Pouncing on her prey
She gives it a fright
Tigress, Tigress
Don't become extinct
Tigress, Tigress
What do you think?
When a hunter comes along,
What do you think?

She looks at her cubs
Clear as day,
Some day they will have to go away
She feels proud, keeps her head up high
Tigress, Tigress.
Don't become extinct
Tigress, Tigress.
What do you think?
When a hunter comes along,
What do you think?

She closes her eyes
Feels someone watching
Ready for attack
She puts her cubs to safety
Tigress, Tigress.
What do you think?
Tigress, Tigress.
When a hunter comes along,
What do you think?

(I think this was the first poem I ever wrote. It was written in November of 1996 and I got a lot of positive comments about it. Along with a lot of encouragement. It was the start of everything and for that I am thankful).

Self-involved people

Self-involved people
Contained in their own selfishness
Only come out of their self-love
To attack you for whatever they project onto you

Self-involved people
Blinder than the pitch black
Deafer than a country night
When the crickets decided to sleep

Self-involved people.
Wrecking balls of pain and destruction
Painting themselves as the victim
Infuriating you
And making you weep.

When you lose a loved one

When you lose a loved one
Your heart doesn't know what to do
Because when you lose a loved one
You think you will never pull through
But that is not true.
Because when you lose a loved one
Your loved one lives in you

Written on 20/5/97

Don't Cry Child

Don't cry child, dry your eyes
Don't fear child, your mother is near
She will hold you in her arms
And make the tears go away
Don't cry child
Even though today is the day
That your father goes away
But don't cry child, everything will be okay

1997.

Poetry

Put a few letters together
You have a word
Something you might not think much of

Put a few words together
You have got a sentence
Something with a meaning

Put a few sentences together
You have poetry
Something that can change you and me

Put some poetry in a book
And you just can't help taking a look

4/7/1997

What I want in my life

In my life
I want to achieve
The contract of record companies
To sit down and write a book
For everyone to take a look

For the man of my dreams to come along
Would give me inspiration for a song
And while I was holding him tight
Nothing else would matter in my life
Wealth and health
For my family, friends and me
Now that would make me happy

To be on the big screen
And watch myself
While eating ice-cream
Would be a dream come true
And live happily ever after
In a mansion for two

Wouldn't you want that too?

29/7/1997

What is interesting about this poem is that it was written before I was even a teenager. Writing tells you something about yourself and it is interesting to note that so many years later I have achieved most of these things. I, like most people I know- well, the women anyway, am very hard on myself. I always feel like I am not achieving enough, or that I have not done enough with my life. Yet, although I did not get a record deal, not only have I published books, this is my fourth. I did find the man of my dreams, married him and had his baby. I have also been on the big screen and watched myself. Though I do not recall whether or not I was eating ice-cream at the time. There is no mansion, only a two-bedroom flat in South-West London, but with property prices how they are, it may as well be. A reminder to be kinder to oneself, I think.

You only notice when things are wrong

I scrape the shell out of the egg
Delicately, with another piece of the shell
It takes me three goes

I dust and cleaned the bathrooms
It took me half a day
You didn't notice
You only notice when things are wrong

Six hundred words of amazing literature
With one spelling mistake
You make no comment but that

When things are going well
Happiness is all there is
And the inability to see
How effective the wheels are
I can't blame you
I only notice things when they are going wrong

Other books by the same author

Acknowledgements.

Thank you to the usual suspects: my mother, Helen. She has always been very supportive of my writing. My husband, James. Margaret Graham who has always been so wonderful. A best-selling writer, she has never pulled the ladder up behind her, only helped so many. Her contribution to so many writer's lives and literature itself is boundless. As ever, to my son Luke: the best thing that ever happened to me. You are everything and more.

About The Author

Catherine Balavage is an author, writer, editor and actor. She is the founder and editor of Frost Magazine. She has been a writer for many years, having her first poem published when she was only 12-years-old. She has written two novels which she is currently editing, and three non-fiction books.

She is also an actress and writes, produces and directs her own films. Catherine lives in South-West London with her husband James, and their son, Luke.